IT'S TIME TO EAT VINE TOMATOES

It's Time to Eat VINE TOMATOES

Walter the Educator

SKB

Silent King Books
A WhichHead Entertainment Imprint

Disclaimer

This book is a literary work; the story is not about specific persons, locations, situations, and/or circumstances unless mentioned in a historical context. Any resemblance to real persons, locations, situations, and/or circumstances is coincidental. This book is for entertainment and informational purposes only. The author and publisher offer this information without warranties expressed or implied. No matter the grounds, neither the author nor the publisher will be accountable for any losses, injuries, or other damages caused by the reader's use of this book. The use of this book acknowledges an understanding and acceptance of this disclaimer.

It's Time to Eat VINE TOMATOES is a collectible early learning book by Walter the Educator suitable for all ages belonging to Walter the Educator's Time to Eat Book Series. Collect more books at WaltertheEducator.com

USE THE EXTRA SPACE TO TAKE NOTES AND DOCUMENT YOUR MEMORIES

VINE TOMATOES

It's time to eat vine tomatoes, so juicy and red,

It's Time to Eat

Vine Tomatoes

Bright little treasures from the garden bed.

Hanging in clusters, they glow in the sun,

A burst of sweet flavor in each little one.

In salads, they sparkle, so shiny and round,

With a taste so fresh, a joy to be found.

Slice them in circles or chop them up small,

They add happy colors that brighten us all.

Their skins are so smooth, their juice is so sweet,

A bite of a tomato is a special treat.

With each little crunch, it's a burst of delight,

Vine tomatoes make every meal feel just right.

On sandwiches too, they sit side by side,

Adding a juicy and tasty red slide.

With cheese or with greens, they're perfect to eat,

Their bright, tangy flavor can't be beat!

It's Time to Eat

Vine
Tomatoes

In pasta, they shimmer, so soft and so warm,

Making sauces rich and giving them form.

Cooked down or fresh, they fill up the dish,

A touch of red magic in every swish.

They love to be roasted, all wrinkled and sweet,

With a flavor that's warm, tender, and neat.

In soups or in stews, they bring such cheer,

Making every spoonful taste better, year by year.

In salsas they're zesty, with onions and spice,

Chopped up and mixed, they taste so nice.

A bowlful of color, a mix fresh and bright,

Vine tomatoes add joy in each bite.

When they're tiny and round, like little red beads,

They're called cherry tomatoes, perfect for feeds.

Pop them in whole, or cut them in half,

It's Time to Eat

Vine
Tomatoes

Their bright little flavor will make you laugh.

Their vines are so twisty, all green and strong,

Helping tomatoes to grow big and long.

Each one is a treasure, so juicy and sweet,

A treat from the garden, tasty to eat.

So next time you see them, give thanks for the vine,

For growing these tomatoes so juicy and fine.

From garden to table, they're here to delight,

It's Time to Eat

Vine
Tomatoes

Making meals tasty, from morning to night!

ABOUT THE CREATOR

Walter the Educator is one of the pseudonyms for Walter Anderson. Formally educated in Chemistry, Business, and Education, he is an educator, an author, a diverse entrepreneur, and he is the son of a disabled war veteran. "Walter the Educator" shares his time between educating and creating. He holds interests and owns several creative projects that entertain, enlighten, enhance, and educate, hoping to inspire and motivate you. Follow, find new works, and stay up to date with Walter the Educator™

at WaltertheEducator.com

9 798330 539710